PLANET PROBLEM SOLVERS

PICK IT UP
A Look at Littering

by Heather DiLorenzo Williams

NORWOOD HOUSE PRESS
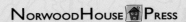

Norwood House Press

For more information about Norwood House Press please visit our website at www.norwoodhousepress.com or call 866-565-2900.
© 2023 Norwood House Press.
All rights reserved. No part of this book may be reproduced or utilized in any form or by any means without written permission from the publisher.

Credits
Editor: Mari Bolte
Designer: Sara Radka

Photo Credits
page 1: ©RealPeopleGroup/Getty Images; page 3: ©dzphotovideo/Getty Images; page 3: ©Westend61/Getty Images; page 3: ©Hill Street Studios/Getty Images; page 5: ©Sawitree Pamee / EyeEm/Getty Images; page 6: ©newannyart/Getty Images; page 8: ©Fuse/Getty Images; page 9: ©Peter Dazeley/Getty Images; page 10: ©Arnuphap Yaiphimai / EyeEm/Getty Images; page 12: ©STORYPLUS/Getty Images; page 13: ©Peter Macdiarmid / Staff/Getty Images; page14: ©Neurone89/Getty Images; page 16: ©Chris Allan/Shutterstock; page 17: ©Taylor Jones/ZUMApress/Newscom; page 19: ©m.malinika/Shutterstock; page 20: ©Maskot/Getty Images; page 22: ©Thomas Winz/Getty Images; page 23: ©Alex Ratson/Getty Images; page 25: ©Allkindza/Getty Images; page 27: ©pixdeluxe/Getty Images; page 29: ©apomares/Getty Images; page 30: ©Gado Images/Smith Collection/Gado/Sipa USA/Newscom; page 31: ©Gado Images/Smith Collection/Gado/Sipa USA/Newscom; page 33: ©Erwin Zwart - Fabrique Computer/The Ocean Cleanup/Cover Images/Newscom; page 34: ©Xavier Subias/agefotostock/Newscom; page 35: ©Ksenia Lokko/Shutterstock; page 36: ©Vidhyaa Chandramohan/ZUMAPRESSNewscom(bottom); page 38: ©P A Thompson/Getty Images; page 39: ©recep-bg/Getty Images(top); page 41: ©Plan Shooting 2 / Imazins/Getty Images(middle); page 43: ©SDI Productions/Getty Images(bottom); page 44: ©Orange Vectors/Shutterstock

Library of Congress Cataloging-in-Publication Data
Library of Congress Cataloging-in-Publication Data has been filed and is available at catalog.loc.gov

Hardcover ISBN: 978-1-68450-782-5
Paperback ISBN: 978-1-68404-744-4

TABLE OF CONTENTS

CHAPTER 1

MAKING A MESS OF THINGS

It is a hot August afternoon in Charlotte, North Carolina. Audrey Scanlon, age 12, and her 10-year-old brother Gregory put on gloves and safety vests. They hold large black garbage bags. Audrey and Gregory pick up trash along the road near their home. Their parents and older siblings help. They find food wrappers and cans and bottles. They even find a diaper or two. Yuck! They work for several hours. Their bags fill with trash.

Audrey and Gregory call themselves the Cleanup Kids. They started seeing trash on the roads and trails around their neighborhood. So they started Clean Sweep. Their group challenges people all over the United States to pick up trash. Every 30-gallon (126.4-liter) bag of trash is a chance to win $250. Audrey and Gregory hope to encourage others to clean up their communities.

Charlotte, North Carolina, is the second-largest city in the southeastern United States. More than 800,000 people live there. More people means more trash. But trash in public places isn't just a problem in Charlotte. It is making a mess of cities and towns around the world.

There are around 6,700 pieces of trash per mile of roadway in the United States. Most pieces are 4 inches (10 centimeters) or less.

What would you do if you saw someone throw trash on the ground?

Trash belongs in garbage bins, bags, or dumpsters. Any kind of trash or waste that is in the wrong place is known as litter. Throwing trash in the wrong place is called littering.

Public places where many people gather are often covered with litter. Beaches and roads are full of litter. It is in stadiums and movie theaters. Litter is usually small amounts of trash that people didn't pick up. French fry bags, soda cans, and cigarette butts are common items. Plastic water bottles, candy and gum wrappers, and straws are others. In fact, most litter is from food and drinks.

Top 10 items found by the International Coastal Cleanup 2019

1 Food wrappers	2 Cigarette butts	3 Plastic bottles	4 Plastic bottle caps	5 Straws and stirrers
4,771,602	4,211,962	1,885,833	1,500,523	942,992

6 Plastic cups & plates	7 Plastic grocery bags	8 Take-out containers	9 Other plastic bags	10 Plastic lids
754,969	740,290	678,312	611,100	605,775

Litter is either intentional or unintentional. Unintentional litter happens by accident. It occurs when trash cans in public places are too full to hold more trash. Sometimes, the wind blows trash from dumpsters or garbage trucks. Animals can even cause unintentional litter. Raccoons, opossums, and even bears like to dig through trash looking for food. The mess they make ends up as litter.

Unintentional litter can be caused by people too. A homeowner might forget to put the lid on their trash can. The wind blows the garbage out, and it ends up on a road or sidewalk. You might drop napkins a fast-food worker gives you in the drive-through line. Gum wrappers or tissues might fall out of your pocket.

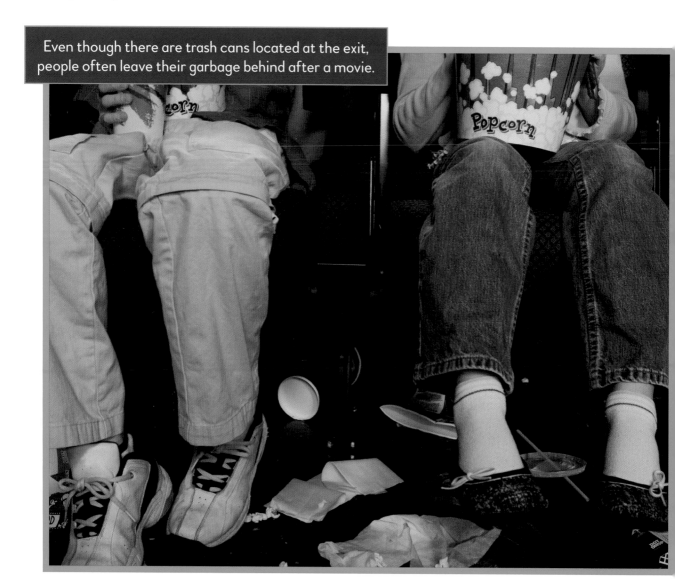

Even though there are trash cans located at the exit, people often leave their garbage behind after a movie.

Intentional litter is a different story. It occurs when people mean to throw trash on the ground. People driving or riding in cars toss litter out their windows. They leave litter behind at parks and zoos. It is found on playgrounds and sports fields. People who litter on purpose are sometimes called litterbugs.

People litter on purpose for different reasons. They might not know where to find a trash can. They feel it's easier to leave their old cups and wrappers behind. Trash cans might be too full. Sometimes, they see others littering, so they think it is okay.

Some people are lazy or careless. They think it's someone else's job to throw away their trash. Others may not understand how litter affects the environment and other people. They might not care. Or they might know that it is wrong, but they don't think it will get them in trouble. No matter what the reason is, a little litter can cause big problems.

Broken glass can be extremely dangerous on beaches and playgrounds. It is easily hidden by sand, which can spread small, sharp pieces.

A lot of litter can ruin a space. The area might smell bad. No one wants to touch, sit on, or step over someone else's trash. A beautiful stream can be ruined by fast-food trash or cigarette butts. A fun day at the playground can be spoiled by garbage from another family's picnic.

Litter can also be unsafe. Metal cans and broken glass are dangerous. These are especially harmful where people like to go barefoot. Discarded cigarettes can lead to huge forest fires. Pets might eat something bad for them.

Insects such as yellow jackets are drawn to garbage. Yellow jackets are stinging wasps that like sugar and rotting meat. And yellow jackets can attack people. They can sting a human over and over again. This can be deadly to anyone allergic to their **venom**. Yellow jackets are a common sight around overflowing trash cans and discarded food.

Wild Waste

Litter is bad news for animals on land too. When squirrels, raccoons, opossums, and other forest critters mistake it for dinner, they can suffer from food poisoning just like humans. Harmful bacteria caused by food contamination can kill some animals. And some trash can cause injuries. Broken glass and sharp metal cans cut inside and out. Containers turn into traps when animals get stuck trying to eat what's left at the bottom. And highway litter often leads animals to busy roadways. They dodge traffic on their quest to check out some tasty trash. But they don't always dodge fast enough.

The amount of unrecycled plastic every year is the same as about 100 plastic bottles per person.

Litter is a big cause of another problem around the world: pollution. Pollution occurs when something harmful is found in the air, soil, or water. Litter can lead to pollution in many ways. On the ground, it can send harmful chemicals into the soil. Plastic bottles release harmful toxins when they are exposed to the sun for a long time. Cigarette butts have chemicals that can poison soil and water.

Food waste also leads to pollution. It begins to rot when it is left on the ground. It attracts bugs and parasites. Old food can breed **bacteria**. Viruses and diseases can spread when people touch this garbage. Animals and insects can also spread diseases.

Littering is bad for the air too. Large amounts of rotting food produce methane. Methane is a **greenhouse gas**. These gases help keep Earth warm. But there is too much food waste in the world. That means there is too much methane. It makes Earth too hot.

Scientists believe around 60 percent of the methane in the atmosphere is caused by human activities, including food waste.

Styrofoam releases toxic chemicals into both the air and the water. It is lightweight and can be carried long distances by wind or waves.

Litter often ends up blowing into open water. Littering causes 60 percent of water pollution. Plastic is one of the biggest causes. Almost 9 million tons (8.2 million metric tons) of plastic ends up in the ocean yearly. Animals think some plastic items are food. Plastic objects can cause internal injuries when animals eat them. And plastic bags and canned drink holders can injure birds, turtles, and other animals.

Plastic breaks down into tiny pieces over time. Fish, turtles, and other sea animals eat up to 24,000 tons (21,772 metric tons) of plastic every year. Humans end up eating some of that plastic too. Scientists believe there is plastic in the fish we eat, the salt we use on our food, and even in our drinking water.

The Great Pacific Garbage Patch is almost three times the size of France. It weighs as much as 500 jumbo jets. But most of the pieces are tiny. They can't be easily picked up and removed. And it is all human-made. It was caused by people. And cleaning it up won't be easy.

Is litter in a park keeping you from using or enjoying playground equipment or the other things at the park? Look around. What is preventing people from keeping things clean?

CHAPTER 2

THE BUSINESS OF CLEANING UP

Highways began to stretch across the US in the 1940s. New roads connected large cities. Traveling between states got easier. More Americans began driving longer distances. Fast-food restaurants soon followed. It became easy to eat on the go. But with fast food came a new problem: litter. Styrofoam cups and containers, paper bags, and plastic straws became common sights along roadways.

Drive-through restaurants have been popular in the US since the first one opened in 1947.

A group of concerned people stepped up. They formed Keep America Beautiful in 1953. The goal was to convince people to clean up roads and communities. They got the message out with signs and television commercials. Volunteer-led cleanups got people helping. School visits taught kids about litter. It was the first group to address litter in the US. Millions of pounds of trash and **recyclables** have been collected since Keep America Beautiful was founded. The group estimates that litter has decreased by 61 percent since 1969.

Today, Keep America Beautiful has more than 700 community groups. They work with schools and businesses. They teach people about the harmful effects of littering. Yearly cleanup days and recycling programs give people ways to help. Volunteers help restore natural areas and parks across the country as well.

Keep America Beautiful is America's largest community improvement group. It has three main goals. Improving recycling in the US and making towns and cities look nicer are two of their goals. But the group's number-one goal is to end littering. They have two litter programs. One is the Great American Cleanup. The other is the Cigarette Litter Prevention Program.

The first Great American Cleanup was in 1998. It takes place for three months every spring. Around 15,000 groups in the US take part. Volunteers pick up trash. They clean up parks, roads, and other public spaces.

The Cigarette Litter Prevention Program wants people to stop throwing cigarette butts on the ground. They work to provide people with places to throw their cigarettes. There are 1,800 communities in the US that use this program.

Keep America Beautiful also gives **grants** to communities. These help people who want to improve their spaces and end littering. They want people to learn about what they can do to help. And they continue to tell the public about littering through ads on TV and online.

Keep America Beautiful supports the idea of **zero-waste** communities too. Rejecting single-use objects, reducing food packaging, reusing products when possible and recycling when not, and composting food waste are all part of a zero-waste future.

THE 5 R'S OF ZERO WASTE

REFUSE

Say no to items that are harmful to the environment, such as straws and plastic shopping bags.

REDUCE

Cut back on the number of packaged items you buy, especially things wrapped in plastic.

REUSE

Buy reusable items such as water bottles and cloth shopping bags, or turn old items into new things.

RECYCLE

Find out what can be recycled in your community and take the time to keep those items out of the trash.

ROT

Turn your food and yard waste into compost—it helps keep the planet healthy and helps your plants grow.

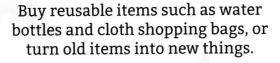

Companies who provide recycling programs for their products are known as circular manufacturers.

But many people think Keep America Beautiful is focusing on the wrong thing. Some think that companies should be more responsible for the items they make. This is known as **circular manufacturing**. It means that companies make less trash. They make more recyclable or reusable products. And they are responsible for recycling their products when people are finished with them. Right now, most people just throw things away when they break. They get something new instead of fixing the old item. If companies helped with recycling and repairs, big changes could be made.

Circular manufacturing is a fairly new idea. But governments have been holding companies more responsible for the environment for several years. Oil spills and poisoned rivers started making the news in the 1960s. Air and water pollution were big problems. Concerned people and politicians took action.

The early 1970s are considered the start of the **environmental movement**. The Environmental Protection Agency (EPA) was formed during this time. The Clean Air Act and Clean Water Act were created too. New rules were written about how factories should get rid of waste. Earth Day was founded in 1970. People began to care more about the land, air, and water around them. They wanted more recycling and less littering.

The first law about littering came about in 1972. Intentional littering is now illegal in all 50 states. Many states have strict laws. Some places such as national parks and beaches have even stricter rules. Fines for littering in a national park can be as high as $5,000. Litterbugs can even go to prison.

Fines for littering are only effective when officials are nearby to catch litterbugs in action.

Litter laws are easier to enforce in national parks. There are park rangers on duty at all times. They keep a watch out for littering. Some parks even have cameras in place. Cameras help rangers catch people who litter. But litter laws in other places are hard to enforce.

Police officers don't always have time to spend on litterbugs. They have bigger crimes to deal with. Sometimes, the litter laws are not clear. This also makes them hard to enforce. People will continue to litter if there is no **consequence**.

What If Everyone Did That?

National Cleanup Day was started by two hikers who were tired of finding trash on park trails. They started out putting the trash they found in their pockets. Then, they carried trash bags on hikes. Other hikers started collecting trash too. Eventually, their hikes turned into a yearly cleanup. People all over the country participate. But the founders hope that people will pick up trash whenever they see it, not just one day a year. They believe that if everyone picked up a piece of trash every day, we would no longer need huge cleanup days. The world would be a lot tidier.

Litter is costly. Cleanup can cost cities millions of dollars each year. Even cities with great trash and recycling programs still deal with it. San Francisco, California, is the country's top recycler. The city's zero-waste goal has changed the way people handle trash. San Francisco keeps 80 percent of the city's waste from **landfills**. People who live there are required to **compost** and recycle.

But some San Francisco neighborhoods still had a litter problem. One former mayor took most of the trash cans out of the city. He believed this would attract less trash. But the trash just ended up on the ground. Concerned citizens had to solve the problem themselves.

Clean Streets was started to deal with the problem. It is a service that picks up trash for a fee. Workers are paid through donations and customer fees. Residents can sign up to have Clean Streets come and tidy up their block. They can also donate money to help with clean-up efforts. The business creates jobs for local residents and keeps neighborhoods cleaner.

Does your family recycle? Compost? How might recycling and composting help with litter in your neighborhood?

If trash dumpsters don't get emptied often enough, they become sources of unintentional litter.

In New Jersey, a group of teens spend the summer cleaning up litter. Jersey City's Department of Recreation has a program called Stop the Drop. Around 180 young people between the ages of 16 and 21 become city employees for the summer. They walk around picking up trash in July and August. The program not only gets rid of litter. It also gives the workers job experience.

Many cities also have programs that give jobs to homeless individuals. One is in San Jose, California. Teams of workers dealing with homelessness have removed 11 million gallons (41.6 million liters) of trash from the city since 2014. In Austin, Texas, an organization that hires homeless people picked up 500 pounds (226.8 kilograms) of trash in one weekend. And in Portland, Oregon, 72 homeless individuals were part of a test program. It provided jobs and got rid of litter. Litter may be measured in different ways. But whether it is counted by bags or pounds, there is a lot of it!

Although littering is illegal, laws are not enough to keep it from happening. People must take responsibility for their waste. And we must create less trash. Manufacturers and the people who buy their products can help stop litter in its tracks.

Where do you see litter the most in your city or neighborhood? On the side of the road? At the park? Somewhere else?

Teens can get valuable work experience from programs like New Jersey's Stop the Drop.

CHAPTER 3

STOPPING LITTER IN ITS TRACKS

Many families visit US beaches each summer. But a day at the beach can be ruined by litter. People leave behind many kinds of litter at the beach. Plastic bottles and lids, straws, and food containers are some examples. They even leave food scraps on the beach sometimes. These items attract seagulls and bugs. And they usually end up blowing into the ocean.

But more than just beaches are affected by litter left behind by tourists. Many amazing spots around the world are overrun with litter. Historical monuments and mountain trails have litter problems too. This costs governments a lot of money. If places are dirty and filled with trash, people might not visit. And no tourists means no income.

Some governments hope to solve this problem with product bans. This means that items that are really harmful can't be used in gift shops, restaurants, or snack bars. Styrofoam, plastic straws, and single-use shopping bags are some examples.

There is so much litter on Kamilo Point in Hawaii that local residents call it Trash Beach.

Packing peanuts and some food containers are made of Styrofoam. These are banned in some countries, states, and large cities. New York State banned Styrofoam in January 2022. Restaurants in some states only give straws to people who ask for them. Some cities have banned all plastic straws. A few states have also outlawed single-use plastic shopping bags. **Biodegradable** or recyclable bags are better options. Paper bags are okay too.

California banned straws in all full-service restaurants in 2019.

WE'VE GONE STRAWLESS

please enjoy our new, better for the environment sip lids!

sip sip hooray!

IF YOU NEED A STRAW, PLEASE ASK A TEAM MEMBER

Take a look around your family's kitchen. What are some items you could stop using and replace with multiple-use items?

Compostable straws are made of plant matter or paper and can be placed into a compost pile with food and yard scraps.

Bans can help keep litter in check. But they won't stop litter from being created. Circular manufacturing can help. Companies would need to change the way they design and make products. Less plastic could be used in making and packing. And any plastic used would be recyclable or compostable. More items could be used again and again instead of thrown away.

Burger King is one company that is trying out circular manufacturing. The fast-food chain is testing reusable sandwich and drink containers. Customers can return them to the restaurant. Workers clean them so they can be used again.

There are many reusable items that can replace single-use plastics. Switching to reusable items could stop litter in its tracks. But we still have to deal with the litter that already exists. Even if single-use plastics disappeared today, the ocean would still be full of trash.

Some companies are using technology to remove trash from the ocean. Ocean Cleanup is an example. It was founded in 2013 by 18-year-old Boyan Slat. Ocean Cleanup made a device that floats in the ocean. It is shaped like a huge U. It is around 0.5 miles (0.8 kilometers) long. Nets attached to the bottom trap trash. Workers remove it once the nets are full.

Ocean Cleanup has already removed 20,000 pounds (9,072 kg) of trash from the ocean. The company believes they can remove 90 percent of the plastic in the ocean by 2040. Ocean Cleanup also removes trash from rivers. Taking trash out of rivers keeps it from reaching the ocean.

Ocean Cleanup's vessels need fuel to run. In 2021, scientists were able to turn ocean plastics into biofuel. That biofuel provides energy for the vessels to continue their work. Using clean energy is another step to protecting the planet.

What's one way you can help clean up litter in your neighborhood?

The plastic gathered by Ocean Cleanup's device is recycled and turned into new items.

Automatic vacuum waste collection systems look similar to regular trash cans.

Litter often ends up on the ground because trash cans are too full. This can happen quickly in crowded areas. Garbage can end up all over the place if workers are not available to empty full trash cans.

In the 1950s, a Swedish company invented pneumatic waste collection systems. *Pneumatic* means "moved by air." These systems are also called automatic vacuum waste collection. They look like regular trash cans. But there are holes in the ground under them. The holes lead to huge tubes. Air pulls trash into the tube like a vacuum cleaner. The trash travels to an underground facility where it is smashed into a cube.

There are several pneumatic systems in Europe, Asia, and the Middle East. But there are not as many in the US. One is at Walt Disney World's Magic Kingdom in Orlando, Florida. The theme park has been using this system since 1971. There is also a pneumatic system on Roosevelt Island in New York City. Since the trash cans are never full, they never overflow. And the area doesn't need garbage trucks since the cans never have to be emptied. This helps the city save money on gas. These automated systems are one way that cities could reduce litter.

Things You Can Do to Help Reduce Litter

STAINLESS LUNCH BOX

SOAP

BRING YOUR OWN CUP

NO PLASTIC BAGS X

RECYCLE IT

SWAP TO A METAL STRAW

GO GREEN

USE GLASS JARS

SAVE THE PLANET

GLASS PAPER PLASTIC

TAKE THE EXTRA STEP TO SORT AND SEPARATE ITEMS THAT CAN BE RECYCLED

RE DUCE USE CYCLE

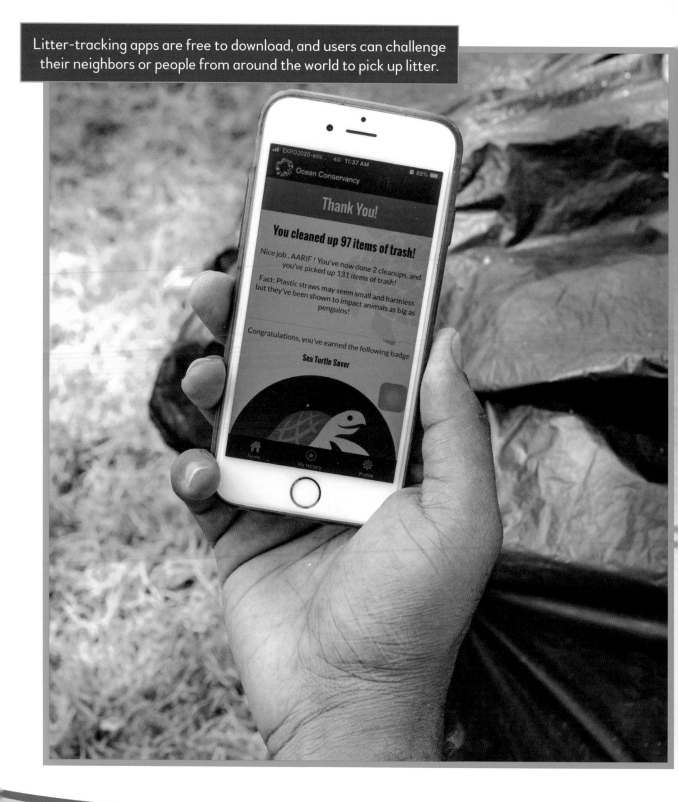

Litter-tracking apps are free to download, and users can challenge their neighbors or people from around the world to pick up litter.

Ocean Cleanup and pneumatic waste collection systems are ways of cleaning up our existing litter. But some groups are using litter that's already out there to convince people not to leave more.

Cities across the US are collecting **data** along with litter. And the scientists who are collecting data are people just like you. These "citizen scientists" pick up litter in their towns, parks, or beaches. They take a picture of each piece they collect. Then, they write descriptions. A smartphone app **geotags** the photo. Each piece of trash goes into a **database**.

Litterati is one of the most popular litter data apps. City leaders, scientists, and environmental experts can use the app's database. It helps them see what kinds of litter are found in an area. The information also helps them understand people's littering habits. This can help them figure out solutions. Maybe more trash cans are needed. Or maybe restaurants in the area should think about banning straws.

Tagging trash with *Litterati* or a similar app solves two problems. It gets litter off the ground and into a trash can where it belongs. It also provides information to help keep more litter from ending up in the same places over and over.

Many places are using this data to create rules and laws. It helps us understand where and when people are more likely to litter. Rangers and officers can keep a closer watch at those times. Enforcing litter laws becomes a bit easier. More trash cans and more "no littering" signs are also helpful. People are more likely to throw their trash away if they have a place to put it. They are also more likely to follow a rule if they see it posted.

Several states are using data to crack down on littering. In Louisiana, the first littering offense is a $900 fine and 16 hours of community service. More littering can lead to going to jail or losing your driver's license. People may think twice about tossing their trash on the ground if they know they will have to pay a fine or go to jail.

But positive reinforcement and friendly contests could also be helpful. Programs like the one Audrey and George Scanlon created give people a chance to win money for picking up litter. And trash collection data apps allow people who live in a community to connect through a shared goal. They can even compete on the app to see who picks up the most trash.

In addition to fines, many states require people who litter to do community service, such as roadside cleanups.

According to Keep America Beautiful, people in the US have picked up more than 0.5 billion pounds (0.2 billion kg) of litter in the past 10 years. They have cleaned more than 500,000 miles (804,672 km) of roads, trails, and waterways. A study shows that all of America's litter would be gone in one day if each person in the country picked up 152 pieces of trash.

Even if all of America's litter disappeared, more would be made. We would have to work together to keep it from piling up again. Anyone can stop litter. We just have to be mindful about what to do with trash in public

Let's Go for a Plog!

You've heard of jogging, but have you ever plogged? *Plogging* means "jogging while picking up litter." It started in Sweden in 2016. Eventually, it made its way to other countries, including the US. Ploggers choose a route, pull on their sneakers, and grab a trash bag. People who don't like to run can even go for a palk (pick up trash while walking) or a pike (pick up trash while hiking). Keep America Beautiful even sponsors TrashDash, a plogging fun run. The September event happens in communities across the country, and people of all ages can participate.

It's also important for homeowners to make sure outdoor trash cans are closed tightly. This prevents it from blowing away or attracting animals.

places. Keeping a trash can or bag in the car gives drivers a place to throw garbage. Park visitors should always carry a trash bag on hikes, picnics, or playdates. Choose reusable items instead of using single-use plastics. Stainless-steel drink containers, reusable straws, and cloth shopping bags are great tools. They keep plastic off the ground, out of landfills, and away from the ocean.

Plogging is a fun way for families to clean up their favorite places and get some exercise at the same time.

One of the most important keys to ending littering is responsibility. Manufacturers and individuals must step up. It is important that we all do our part to take care of the planet. Programs in schools, communities, and businesses help teach people about why littering is harmful.

Kids are leading the way. When Audrey and George Scanlon started Clean Sweep, they used their own allowance to fund the first prize. Since then, local businesses and individuals have started helping them. People who are inspired by the program are now funding the prize. Audrey and George are not just cleaning up their hometown. They are making others aware of the problem. The people who hear their message get inspired to do something about it.

Although littering has decreased in the US over the past several years, we have a long way to go. From state laws to neighborhood cleanups, and from smart trash cans to citizen science, we can all work together to put trash in its place.

Littering is a problem people of all ages can help solve.

Why do you think people litter?

Activity 1:

Create "No Littering" signs for a place you visit often—a neighborhood park, your community pool, or even the school playground. Remember, people are less likely to litter if there's a sign nearby asking them not to!

MATERIALS:

- access to the internet
- poster board
- markers
- tape

PROCEDURE:

1. In your school library or at home, use the internet to research litter ad campaigns. This will give you some ideas. "Give a hoot—don't pollute!" is one example.

2. Create your own ad campaign. You might choose to use an animal or insect character. Or you might pick a word or phrase you like.

3. Make enough signs to hang in the space you have chosen.

Activity 2:

Plan a plog, palk, or pike in your school community! Challenge each class at your school to pick up the most trash.

MATERIALS:
- access to the internet
- trash bags
- gloves

PROCEDURE:
1. With your teacher's help, choose a date. It could be during the school day, or on a Saturday so families can participate. You may even want to register for Keep America Beautiful's Trash Dash, which takes place in September each year. (https://kab.org/kab-events/trashdash/event/).

2. Decide where your participants will collect trash, and how long they will have. Thirty minutes is a great place to start.

3. On the day of your event, hand out trash bags and gloves to each team.

4. Ready, set, plog!

GLOSSARY

BACTERIA (bak-TEER-ee-uh): germs

BIODEGRADABLE (BY-oh-duh-GRAY-duh-buhl): able to be broken down by nature

CIRCULAR MANUFACTURING (SIR-kyoo-luhr man-yoo-FAK-shuhr-ing): a system of making things that focuses on less waste and more recycling

COMPOST (KOM-pohst): to mix food and yard waste together with soil to create a natural fertilizer called humus

CONSEQUENCE (KON-suh-kwens): the result of an action or behavior

DATA (DAY-tuh): information

DATABASE (DAY-tuh-bays): a collection of information stored in a computer

ENVIRONMENTAL MOVEMENT (en-vy-ruh-MEN-tuhl MOOV-muhnt): a worldwide effort involving multiple people, activist groups, and government organizations to address issues related to nature and the health of the planet

GEOTAGS (GEE-oh TAYGS): to add information about location to a picture or other file on the internet

GRANTS (GRANTS): sums of money given to someone in order to fund a project or solve a problem

GREENHOUSE GAS (GREEN-hows GAS): a substance in Earth's atmosphere that traps heat energy from the sun

LANDFILLS (LAND-fills): places where garbage is buried

RECYCLABLES (ruh-SY-kluh-buhls): items that can be turned into reusable material

VENOM (VEN-uhm): a type of poison that some animals make and inject into other animals or people by stinging or biting

ZERO-WASTE (ZEE-roh WAYST): waste prevention that encourages responsible production, use, and reuse of items, with the goal of sending no waste to the landfill

FOR MORE INFORMATION

BOOKS

French, Jess. *What a Waste: Trash, Recycling, and Protecting Our Planet.* New York, NY: DK Publishing, 2019.

Hilton, Hélène, ed. *Recycle and Remake.* New York, NY: DK Publishing, 2020.

Thomas, Isabel. *This Book Is Not Garbage: 50 Ways to Ditch Plastic, Reduce Trash, and Save the World!* New York, NY: Random House Children's Books, 2021.

WEBSITES

Kids Go Green: Litter and Our Oceans

https://pbslearningmedia.org/resource/ee18-sci-waterpol/kids-go-green-litter-and-our-oceans/
Follow the journey of an aluminum can as a piece of litter in the ocean.

Litter Facts

https://worldschildrensprize.org/litterfacts
Learn about litter—especially plastics—and its effect on the planet.

The Problem with Plastic Pollution

https://www.natgeokids.com/uk/kids-club/cool-kids/general-kids-club/plastic-pollution/
Discover the effects of litter on the oceans and how it gets there.

INDEX

ABOUT THE AUTHOR

Heather DiLorenzo Williams is a writer and educator with a passion for seeing readers of all ages connect with others through stories and personal experiences. She enjoys running, reading, and watching sports. Heather lives in North Carolina with her husband and two children.